AF488315

NORTH STAR

Yashvi Shah

(Harmony)

BookLeaf Publishing

India | USA | UK

North Star © 2024 Yashvi Shah

All rights reserved.

No part of this publication may be reproduced, stored in a retrieval system, or transmitted, in any form or by any means, electronic, mechanical, photocopying, recording, or otherwise, without the prior permission of the author.

Yashvi Shah asserts the moral right to be identified as the author of this work.

Illustrations by Yashvi Shah

Presentation by BookLeaf Publishing

Web: www.bookleafpub.com

E-mail: info@bookleafpub.com

ISBN:9789363315907

First edition 2024

To make my father proud, and mother happy.

ACKNOWLEDGEMENT

I owe immense gratitude to those who've made this book possible. Social media, often criticized, has been my guiding light. Through Threads, Instagram, and YouTube, kind strangers nurtured my writing, offering love, appreciation, and guidance. They shared their heartfelt sentiments, allowing me to craft them into works of art, and helped build a community that enriched my understanding of diverse emotions. Grateful for everyone who connected with @shahyashvii and inspired this journey.

Special thanks to BookLeaf Publishing for their 21-day challenge, which transformed nearly 100 poems into this collection.

My gratitude extends further to George Sir and Pronoy Sir, whose mentorship enhanced this work. To Kaplnaben, Rose, and Amrit Sir (Spandan), your encouraging words bolstered my confidence in writing. Heartfelt thanks to Tamanna and Amrit Sir for their poignant preface. And to my father, you know how much your support means to me; I couldn't have done this without you.

FOREWORD

It is my privilege to introduce Yashvi Shah Harmony, a young and passionate poet whom I met just a month ago at our literary program. I believe Yashvi is destined to earn recognition in the field of English literature.

Upon delving into her anthology, North Star, I found myself particularly impressed by the second and third sections. The second section beautifully portrays her acceptance of loneliness and whatever destiny brings, whether to stay or leave.

The third section showcases her reflections on relationships and life's hardships, suggesting a deep understanding gained through personal experience. It is clear she has encountered life's darker aspects intimately yet remains introspective and resilient in the face of these challenges.

This anthology highlights Yashvi Shah Harmony's literary prowess, keen observation, and insight into the complexities of modern life. It is a testament to her talent and depth, promising a bright future in literature.

Amrit Maheshwari "Spandan,"
Author of 8 books in 4 different languages

Hi! Have you ever come across a literary piece that touched you to the core and felt like a warm hug on a rainy evening? North Star is that warm hug for me. Each poem is built upon a different emotion, but what chains them all together is the self-reflection of thoughts.

While reading the anthology, my eyes landed on some lines that my mind knew would be stuck in my heart, so I marked some verses to come back to when I felt down. Every bit of the verse is full of life and beauty.

And when talking about beauty, how can one forget the exquisite illustrations? I was taken aback when I was told that the illustrations were designed by the author herself. It made me wonder about the wide horizon of imagination she possesses.

I believe one must read this book if they are not into poetry, and I strongly believe one must devour this book if one is into poetry. For those who are not into poetry, pick it up, and read it—I know you are going to love it, for it pierces straight into the heart.

Tamanna Sharma,
"Whispers From A Grave"

"Although I'm not an English reader, North Star didn't feel like a foreign language; it spoke to me effortlessly. The innovative index with demarcation of feelings is something I haven't seen in other books. Yashvi's expression is amazingly crisp and crystal clear. Her vast yet simple vocabulary appeals to the reader. Her narration in 'I like my pace, Read between the lines, Pause is not escaping, I am a pawn' makes readers feel connected to her thoughts. Yashvi has a poetic heart that pierces the feelings of readers. Wishing her lots of success and more writing."

- Maya Desai, Mumbai

"Publishing a volume of verse is like dropping a rose petal down the Grand Canyon and waiting for the echo. North Star seems like a beautiful effort. I am proud of Yashvi for sharing the essence of her thoughts and expressions."

- Jayshree Patel, Vadodara

"North Star" is a collection in which the various sensations, feelings, difficulties, and practical shocks of life are shown easily. Each chapter leads the reader to a different dimension of realization, showing emotions easily and naturally.

-Dilip Dholakia "Shyam"
Poet, Junagadh

The art of writing such beautiful compositions is called Maa Saraswati's blessing. Yashvi's poems have beautifully described what we often don't understand, prompting us to question, "What are we really doing?"

-Arati Ramani "Angel"
Bangalore

Table of Contents

ACCEPT

CHERISH

REALIZE

Thanks to Reality

I was a people's person.
Now I am a pen-and-paper one.

I was a laughter person.
Now I am the silent one.

I was a playful river shore.
Now I am quite an ocean one.

I was a morning person.
Now I am a night owl one.

I was a happy person,
Now I am just a pretentious one.

Tortured Talent

Normal humans are blessed with youth,
I am tortured with regrets.

Normal humans are blessed with loans,
I am tortured with privilege.

Normal humans are blessed with mediocrity,
I am tortured with talents.

Normal humans are blessed, and on the
contrary,
I am tortured for being extraordinary.

So Little

We write so much,
but we mean so little.

We read so much,
but we understand so little.

We feel so much,
but we love so little.

We crave so much,
but we appreciate so little.

We sleep so much,
but we dream so little.

We live so much,
but we are alive so little.

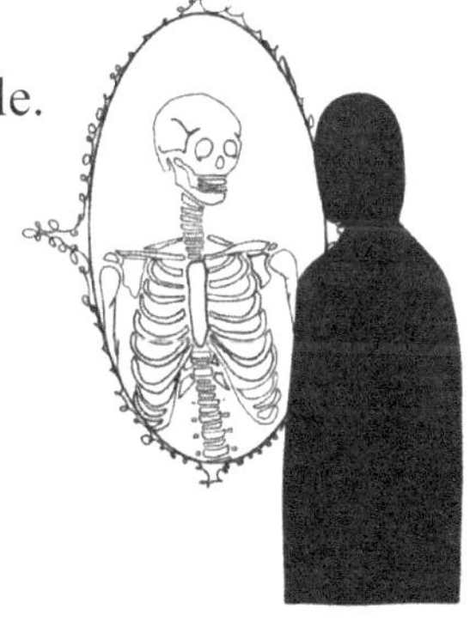

Nothing Anymore

I am surrounded by loved ones,
but hardly feel loved anymore.

I talk to people every day,
but hardly feel I am being heard anymore.

I work my part every day,
but hardly feel I am getting anywhere
anymore.

I smile everyday, every moment,
but hardly cherish anything anymore.

I Realized…

I thought
I'm an artist,
only to realize
I'm an amateur.

I thought
I was learning,
only to realize
I am naive.

I thought
I was happy,
only to realize
I forgot my sorrows.

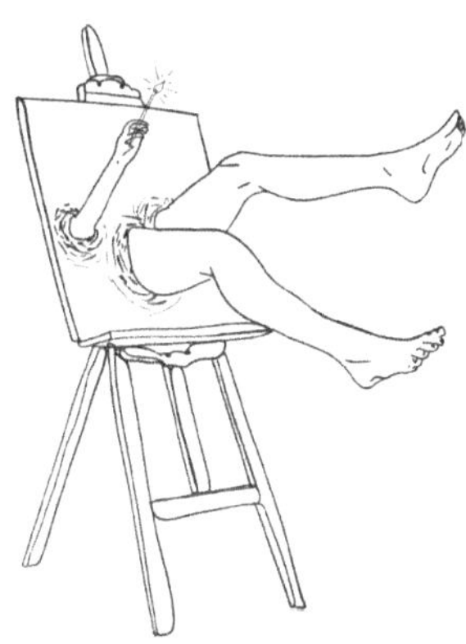

I thought
I was alone,
only to realize
I was lonely.

Lost Victory

I can call myself successful now,
But I have nobody to celebrate with.

I have so many jokes now,
But I have nobody to laugh with.

I have tears in my eyes now,
But I have nobody to wipe them.

I am in so much pain now,
But I have nobody who cares.

I have so much love to share,
But I have no "loved one" anywhere.

I think none of this is even necessary,
As long as I have a pen and my diary.

I Don't Fit In…

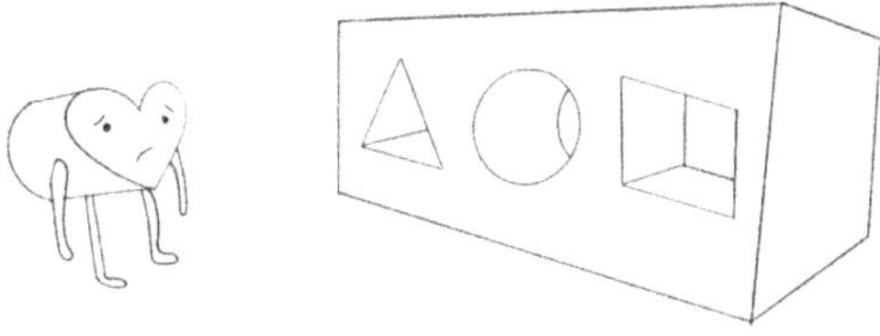

Am I too sensitive,
Or are they born as a rock?

Am I missing something,
Or are they just ahead of their time?

Am I too dumb,
Or are they too intelligent?

Am I too emotional,
Or are they naturally detached?

Am I too kind of a person?
Or arc they simply cruel?

Am I a normal human,
Or are they gamblers of emotions?

I am not sure what it is...
But whatever it is...
I am sure,
I don't fit in!

I am Exhausted

I am exhausted with ideas.
I am exhausted with plans.
I am exhausted without even working.
I am exhausted by the mistakes I'm making.
I am exhausted with this day.
I am exhausted at night.
I am exhausted to feel.
I am exhausted to touch.
I am exhausted to live.
I am exhausted so much.

Grateful Yet Sad

I know I have reasons to smile
But I don't feel like it anymore.
I know I have reasons to be grateful
But I don't feel like it anymore.
I know I have duties to fulfill
But I don't feel like doing them anymore.
I am tired of this empty feeling
But I don't feel like feeling it anymore.

A Little Bit More

The way you enjoy your life
Makes me envy you a little bit more.

The way you are so grounded and bound to
rules
Makes me push my boundaries a little bit
more.

The way you are so strong and fearless
Makes me feel secure a little bit more.

The way you are so focused
Makes me distracted a little bit more.

The way you cry over little things
Makes my heart smile a little bit more.

I know we don't have much time together,
But all I pray for is just
A little bit more...

You, Me and Moon

They say we can't have heaven on earth,
But we can have you, me, and daisies.

They say we can't have heaven on earth,
But we can have you, me, and coffee.

They say we can't have heaven on earth,
But we can have you, me, and the moon.

They say we can't have heaven on earth,
But we can have you, me, and snow.

They say we can't have heaven on earth,
But who needs heaven when we have
you and me?

You Are My Everything

When I am sick, you are my pills.

When I am drowning, you are my gills.

When I am frowning, you are my smiles.

When I am a wanderer, you are my miles.

When I am in darkness, you are my moon.

When I am a caterpillar, you are my cocoon.

When I am a fainted lion, you are my roar.

When I am lost at sea, you are my shore.

You "Were" Mine

It was evening when
I realized you weren't mine.

I did not know what was to come,
But I indeed skipped to dine.

Following all the days and nights,
I smiled, pretending to be fine.

Even in the most vulnerable moments,
I was grateful, that for a significant time,

I was yours,
And you were mine.

My Mind Has Other Plans

I am at rest,
But my mind has other plans.

I am at my best,
Yet my mind has other plans.

I am grateful for what's around me,
Still, my mind has other plans.

I have so much to execute,
However, my mind has other plans.

I know I am alive,
But, my mind has other plans.

I Like My Pace

I ponder as
I lift my pen and
I write my thoughts,
I find them in Italics, but

They force me to be bold
They judge my thoughts
They tell my words are worthless
They push through the cliff till

I am about to give up
I suffer in silence, as
I am not allowed to express my thoughts.
I happen to experiment, and

They don't like it, as
They can't relate to beauty
They don't welcome reality
They want to live life in grief, but

I write with grace
I like my pace, and
I believe that

I am living and
They are just alive.

Your People

You don't need a mic,
To be heard by
your people.

You don't need a lens,
To capture the happiness with
your people.

You don't need an amplifier.
To think out loud among
your people.

You don't need a radio,
To tune in with
your people.

Because if you need assistance,
To spend time with
your people,

Think again, as they
might not be
your people.

Stuck

Each day the universe is expanding,
But I am stuck in these white walls.

Each day seasons are changing,
But I am stuck with these resentful eyes.

Each day people are succeeding,
But I am stuck with this fear of failure.

Each day I go around and do my part,
As I am stuck in this life without art.

Choice

When life offers a choice between two,
Take time to ponder what you want to
pursue.

You may find neither path is wrong,
But choose the one where you truly belong.

So Slow, Oh So Fast

Days pass so slow,
Yet years pass so fast.

Sorrows pass so slow,
Yet tears pass so fast.

Dreams pass so slow,
Yet youth passes so fast.

Success passes so slow,
Yet efforts pass so fast.

Love passes so slow,
Yet loved ones pass so fast.

I Want To Know

It's been so many years
since I've been working,
But I want to know
when did it all stop working?

It's been so many years
since I've been smiling,
But I want to know
when did I start to fake it?

It's been so many years
since I've been loving,
But I want to know
when did I stop feeling loved?

It's been so many years
since I've been alive,
But I want to know
when did I stop living?

Losing to Win

We discovered we are intelligent
And made one person's ability a quotient.

We found we are smart
And decided to make others likewise.

We found we can be better
And boarded the never-ending race.

But here we are,

Losing our minds to match
Another mind's intelligence.

Losing our patience
To make our kids the best.

Losing our money
To make easy money.

Losing our comfort zone
To get comfortable in the future.

Losing ourselves
To find a new self within us.

Read Between The Lines

There's a line between
Love and lust,
Observe the line carefully

There's a line between
Hatred and criticism,
Observe the line carefully

There's a line between
Ambition and greed,
Observe the line carefully

There's a line between
Happiness and pleasure,
Observe the line carefully

They tell me to
Observe these lines carefully,

And now when I have
memorized all the lines

They ask me to
Read between the lines, carefully.

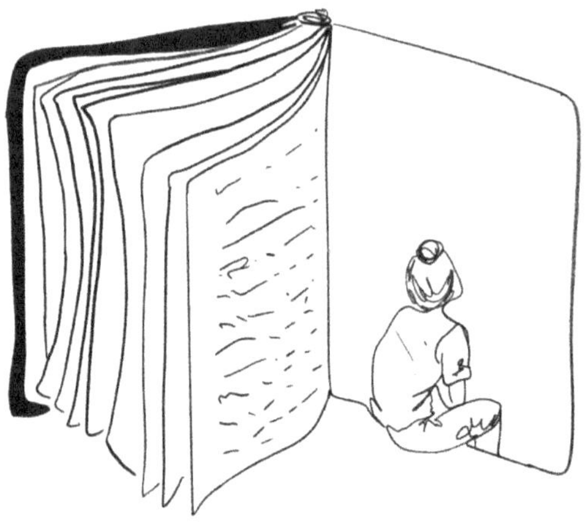

Choose Humanity

God gave us eyes
To appreciate sunshine,
Not for tears at night.

God gave us lips
To speak love,
Not to make love without feeling it.

God gave us arms
To comfort loved ones,
Not to raise them against children.

God gave us fingers
To write history,
Not to point at our ancestors.

God gave us a brain
To empathize with the needy,
Not to take advantage of them.

Maybe you don't believe in God—
But we have a sound mind to decide,

To choose things in favor of humanity,
Not to be cruel and take pride.

Petty And Helpless

Then there are times
Of extreme illness,

Surrounded by nothing but
Grief and darkness.

Moments we lived in the past
Are now oh so lifeless.

Days we spent in the rat race
Seem nothing but meaningless.

Not having sorrow
Is itself a sense of happiness.

Never have humans
found themselves petty and helpless.

Coffee Stains

Coffee stains map the table,
As I keep my head busy with work.

This helps in many ways,
One is the bank, one is my mind.

Keeping too many tabs open on the laptop,
Makes me avoid that void in my heart.

I am tired and wrap things up soon,
and my mind is wide awake.

Thanks to the coffee-stained desk,
Now I am up all night, with heavy eyes.

I seek some peace,
All I could find was pleasure.

I might be pampered with worldly measures
But now I seek the real treasure.

Falter And Hide

Cities exhibit life's facade,
Empty souls in the restless charade.

Avid dreamers are in the rat race,
Restless hearts can't find a comfort space.

Lips seek lips for love and grace,
Frowning within without leaving a trace.

Arms extend to comfort and embrace,
Loneliness dwells in, that's another case.

Pens that write poems are washed city tide,
Reside forgotten in the drawer's side.

Rooms filled with people to celebrate grand stride,
And as the party ends they falter and hide.

Maybe, You Are The ONE?

My hair is loose,
so is my soul.
You take my hand,
my heart follows along.
My feet dance on their own,
so does my inner child.
You share all your secrets,
Damn, so dark and wild.
You compliment my smile knowing
how hard it is for me to have one.
My little mind comprehends,
Signals, maybe you are the one?

ACCEPT

Mirror Of The Society

Look how I was
doing so well,
by myself.

But look how I am
now compared with peers
and unsatisfied with myself.

Look how I found
solace in my work.
But then they said,
"You need to make a few
more bucks from your work."

Look how I was
happy in those beloved arms

But then they said,
"You need more than
love and charm."

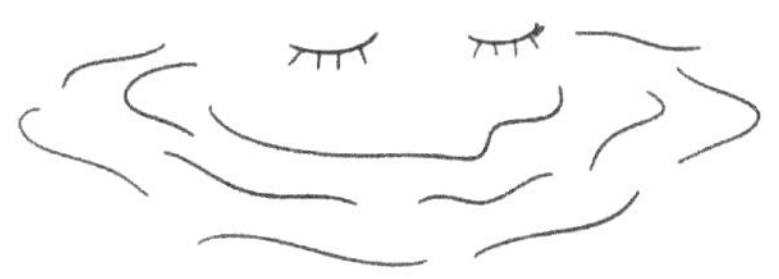

The Gray Patch

Am I
Alone?
Or lonely?

Am I
Healing myself?
Or killing myself?

Am I
Growing up?
Or stuck in place?

Am I
Learning to swim??
Or drowning to death??

Am I
Coming together?
Or breaking apart?

Am I
Moving forward?
Or running away?

Am I
Silent and wise?
Or simply unheard?

Am I
Strong handling the life?
Or just pretending to be?

Am I
Lucid dreaming?
Or escaping reality?

Am I
Living my life?
Or merely existing?

To Keep Myself Sane

I feel more than fact,
I react more than act.

I love more than life,
And it hurts more than a
knife.

I think of everyone around,
But here I am left with frowns.

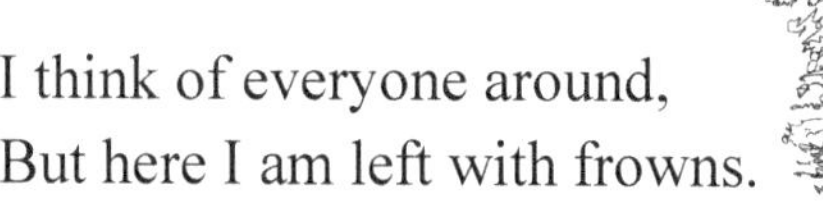

"Think of a bright future," they say,
But all I can see is black, white, and gray.

I can't help my brain;
All my efforts are in vain.

I have no choice,
But to write all of my pain,

As that's the only way
To keep myself sane.

Paradox

I need to learn so much,
I need to unlearn some as well.

I need to experience so much,
I need to forget some as well.

I need to feel so much,
I need to heal from some as well.

I need to leave so much,
I need to be there for some as well.

I need to love so much,
I need to move on from some as well.

I need to live so much,
I need to die a little as well.

Endless Pursuits

I am cursed with
Too many dreams.

I have tried like seventeen things,
Which means sixteen are incomplete.

This gives them a reason to laugh,
And my loved ones to scream.

However, here I am,
Trying out an eighteenth thing.

I am not sure if I'll succeed,
But I know I'll bloom.

Regardless of whether
It's autumn or spring.

Bound to Rules

They tell me to go beyond the stereotypes,
But being in peace is where I strive.

They try to fit me in black and white,
Although they know I am colorful.

They ask me to share my views,
And then laugh and call me old school.

I don't care as my day often ends with a
smile.
On this land adorned with idiots,

I think of myself as a smarter fool.
They tell me to break stereotypes,

I see myself bound to rules.

Faraway Foreign

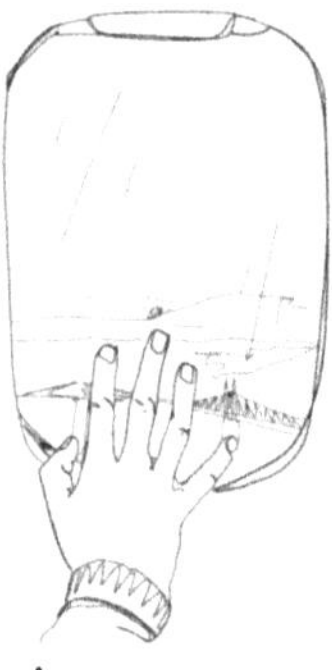

I see people surviving,
But I dream of living.

I see people existing,
But I dream of experiencing.

I see people happy,
But I dream of pleasures.

I see people satisfied,
But I dream of being restless.

I see people grounded,
But I dream of leaving this ground.

I see people love the natives,
But I dream of hating the foreign.

Journey of Seasons

The day changes its breeze,
The sky changes its colors,
The moon changes the sea,

And look how fate
Changed us to lovers.

But here's the curious thing about fate:

The day still changes every day,
The sky paints a new canvas every day,
The moon brings a new shape every day,

And oh, we changed
Little by little,

Every day.

To Feel

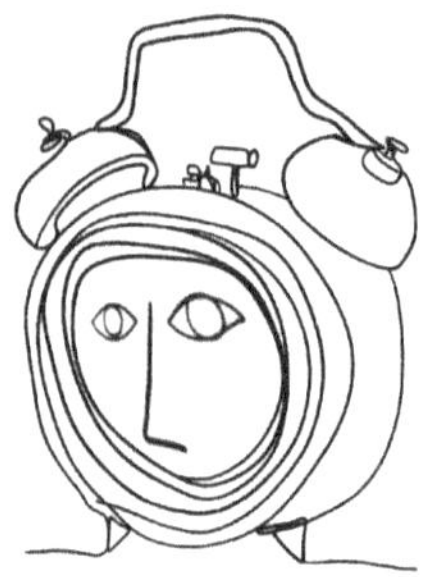

Sometimes life moves so fast,
I don't have time to feel.

Sometimes life moves so slow,
I still can't heal.

Sometimes life gives so much hate,
I confuse it with love.

Sometimes life gives so much love,
I feel like the almighty above.

Sometimes I want to sit and write,
To express all the things I feel.

But again, sometimes life moves so fast,
I don't have time to feel.

Pause Is Not Escaping

Take a pause,
Feel the chaos.

Settle a bit,
You are not here to quit.

Accept the situation,
Find a solution.

If there's a storm, bend.
This is not the end.

You are not at your best,
Take some rest.

Pause is not escaping,
It's healing.

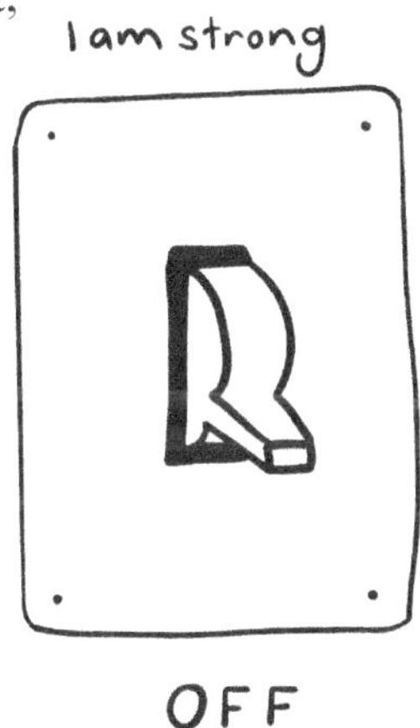

Horizons

Horizons are interesting,
Making us believe in delusion.

They actually never meet,
But create a romantic illusion.

When the sea and sky
Kiss each other at the end of the day,

Even the burning sun
Feels cute and melts away.

And here we are,
Busy fulfilling mundane duties,

Hardly lifting our heads
To adore the world's beauty.

Everyday, But Not Every Day

Fire burns every day,
But it feels nice only in winter.

Home is there every day,
But feels like home only in sorrows.

Nights occur after every day,
But feel long with overthinking.

Eyes can observe every day,
But observe only when the mind allows.

Creativity can flow every day,
But it only does when the environment is
nice.

We can fall in love every day,
But we do only when destiny decides.

How To Dream

I have been in a cage for so long
That I have forgotten how to dream.

I have been this bored for so long
That I now enjoy my coffee with cream.

I have been this busy for so long
That I now see clearly in shower steam.

I have been lonely for so long
That my lips are silent and my heart
screams.

I have been this plain for so long
That dark academia is not my theme.

I have been this obedient for so long
That I want to go high and
Do something extreme.

Hope, You Are Worth It

Dear Future,

Hope you are worth
All the butterflies I imagine.

Hope you are worth
All the tears I shed today.

Hope you are worth
All the efforts that seem in vain.

Hope you are worth
All the regrets I never reveal.

Hope you are worth
All the sacrifices I have made.

Hope you are worthy
To survive this meaningless life.

Deprived Necessity

Flowers need season to bloom,
Artists need inspiration to create,
Poets need a muse to pen,
And I need you to survive.

But now,

I need to live without falling for you,
Flowers need to bloom in fall too,
Artists need to earn money too,
Poets need to pen without loving too.

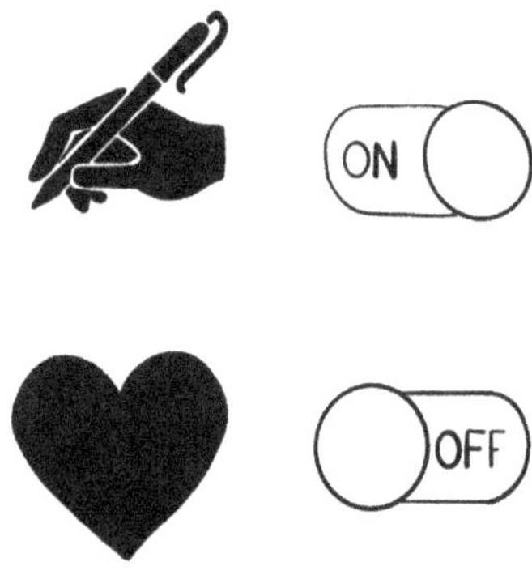

Mine And Yours

Waves are fine,
Sand is coarse.

Sky is mine,
Land is yours.

I am tired,
Yet doing my chores.

I am in momentum,
Not sure what's the force.

Surviving with a smile,
Ignoring all the chaos.

No matter how much I try,

These tears are mine,
As I cannot be yours.

Skeptic Instead

I think I am a firm decision-maker,
But you make me weak instead.

I think I am skilled at being independent,
But you make me sick of it instead.

I think I can walk alone well,
But you make me critique instead.

I think I can express myself well,
But you easily trick me instead.

I think I'll find some love again,
But you make me a skeptic instead.

The Inevitable

Okay, if you say so,

I'll erase all the pictures we had.
But what about the impression
You left on my heart?

Okay, if you say so,

I'll discard and disregard all the gifts.
But what about the disputes we had
That are now ingrained in my genes?

Okay, if you say so,

I'll delete all the voice memos we
exchanged.
But what about your sweetest melody
That keeps resonating in my ears?

Fading Memories

The love, the care,
The tears, the pain,
The arms, the secrets,
The wounds, the weakness.

I remember each bit,
Every freaking moment of time.
But now that's all in the past,
I can't help but age with time.

The memories are fading,
The wounds are healing,
The scars are leaving,
The eyes are drying.

I am scared that,
A day will come,
When my mind won't recall you.
A night will come,
When my eyes won't cry for you.

Ironic Utopia

I want freedom in a cage,
No wrinkles when I age.

I want to record each day on a page,
Except for a few years of my teenage.

I juggle between love and rage,
And often feel empty—how strange.

I crave new things, but fear change,
Outperforming always, as the world's a
stage.

I spent my life gathering all the knowledge,
Only to realize half is not acknowledged.

They call me fortunate, as I am privileged,
And dismiss my efforts as mere garbage.

Equilibrium

If my life is classical mechanics,
What I lack is equilibrium.

Equilibrium between
Day and night,

Equilibrium between
Sleep and dreams,

Equilibrium between
Chasing your dreams
Or
Chasing your dream girl,

Equilibrium between
Time with loved ones
Or
Time spent practicing what you love.

And say, if magically I find
An equilibrium,

I will find myself
Missing out on maximum,
As, fortunately, I am
Cursed as a human.

61

To Look Back

Those days were better,
When the room was a mess,
Yet thoughts were clear.

Those days were better,
When cash was better less,
Yet smiles were more.

Those days were better,
When tears were more,
Yet frowns were less.

Those days were better,
When sleep was more,
Yet dreams were less.

I might feel sadness,
Yet gratitude fills my heart,
The memories I hold are nothing less than
art.

A Reminder

Appreciate the blessings now,
What's the point of it after expiry?

Appreciate your loved ones now,
What's the point of it after death?

Appreciate your health now,
What's the point of it after youth?

Appreciate your thoughts now,
What's the point once you're asleep?

Appreciate your surroundings now,
What's the point after isolation?

I see some of these might
not be worthy to be appreciated.
Appreciate them,
not because they are worthy to be,

But because you still have
the ability to appreciate them.

Just Like AI

Year of 2022
As Artificial Intelligence
Disrupts our daily lives,

It makes me wonder
And finally realize—

Just like AI,
I also,
Don't ask and question,
But only follow.

Just like AI,
I am running through life,
Rapid, fast, and quick,
And similarly, I don't feel
A single thing.

Just like AI,
I am working
Day and night.
Neither do I celebrate
Nor ever pick a fight.

Just like AI,
I hardly feel
Smart or dumb.
This world has made
My feelings go numb.

I am afraid.
If this is how
The world will be,
Will those be humans
When we refer to "we"?

As I think and
Try to understand,
I am given
Another command.

And hereby,

I do what I am told,
Have a price tag and get sold.

Thankfully, these words
Are not written by AI.

So, if you could relate to the poem—
Congratulations,
You are still human,
Not AI.

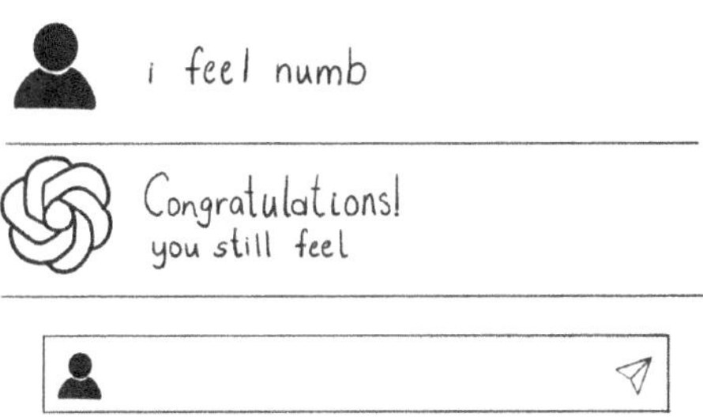

Accept My Reality

I accept
All the things around me

The harsh warmth of an Indian afternoon,
The confused colors of the evening,

Sheer darkness of night regardless of moon,
And everything between the end and
beginning.

I have been trying to change my life,
But all I could change was my perspective.

I can't seem to change the story,
Though I attempt to shift the narrative.

I'll fulfill my dream before
being embraced by mortality.

But today,
I accept my reality.

CHERISH

Take A Deep Breath

The storm has gone,
The sun will rise.

You've come this far,
You are surely wise.

Though clouds may linger
Around for sometime,

Know there's a long while
Before another storm arrives.

Hopelessly Hopeful

Perhaps my stars are not aligned,
But I am still hopeful when I look at the
sunset.

Perhaps my fate is not filled with love,
But my heart still craves to share the love.

Perhaps my days are not the best,
But I bet I am trying to be my best.

Perhaps my nights are lonely today,
But I am wide awake as I refuse to accept
my today!

Perhaps, they are right,
I am not taking care of myself,
But there's not a moment
when I don't worry about them.

Keep Being Wise

I'll travel the world if I can,
Or read all the words ever written in the
clan.

I'll experience all the love with my man,
Or read and cherish every man written by
women.

I'll meet a person of every culture,
Or read about them in ancient scripture.

I'll die as a person with experience,
And nobody can convince me otherwise.

I am digging a tunnel till my fortunes rise,
Till then I'll read, keep being wise.

Somebody's Own World

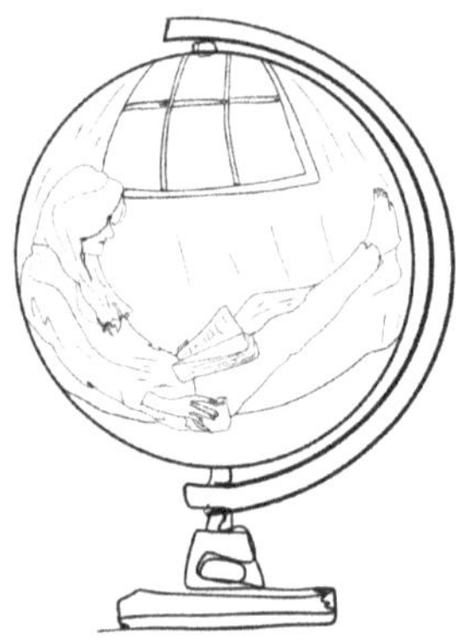

With a vanilla candle,
A cozy corner becomes
Somebody's own world.

A bunch of relatives,
Giggling and having snacks,
A vivid room of emotion becomes
Somebody's own world.

A seaside office,
With an amazing team,
Taking a dream to a startup becomes
Somebody's own world.

A night of passion,

In loving arms,
Eyes that seek love and care becomes
Somebody's own world.

There is a place that awaits,
Where the heart will be happy,
And you could call it
Your own world.

Happiness Is A Decision

A kid is happy
to get a new bicycle with clutches,
another kid is happy
to walk without crutches.

An aunt is happy
to have her son back from the borders,
another is happy
to send her son to study abroad.

A daughter is happy
to marry her love,
another is happy
to raise her child alone.

Everybody has a different story;
I like to believe, a happy one.

Because happiness is not a gift from God,
Happiness is a decision.

Denied Abundance

Isn't it amazing how

when a flower can make you smile
But a garden cannot?

When a pastel sky can make you happy
But a rainbow cannot?

When a sweet tooth can make you happy
But a course of meal cannot.

When a scrap of poem can make you happy
But a grand library cannot.

When a fictional character can give giggles
But that special one cannot.

Isn't it amazing how…

When scarcity is desired
But abundance is denied.

Flawless But Imperfect

Let's take a deep breath
and try to recollect,
Whether you are an engineer,
doctor, artist, or architect,

All the world ever called
you was "Imperfect",
Questioning elders,
might be seen as disrespect.

Each person is taught
from childhood that,
"Be a person that
nobody can reject."

As we grow, we chase
money, fame, and respect,
Only to find that,
life's pieces are incorrect.

Soon, we realize all the
pieces of life are incorrect,
And a question mark

is all that's left!

Soon, we experience anxiety,
depression, or a panic attack,
Sometimes we seek therapy,
sometimes pills, often just a small nap.

And all a person can do,
with the question mark is to neglect;
Very soon, these questions,
cease to affect.

After all,
we humans are mirrors;
We reflect,
what the world incidents.

The mirror finally breaks,
for not being as they expect.
We take the broken pieces,
and try to reconnect.

After all the chaos,
we tend to conclude,
We may become flawless,
but will always be imperfect!

Accept And Improve

I have messy hair,
Sometimes I like its curls,
Sometimes they get on my nerves.

I like my toothy smile,
Sometimes it makes me look unique,
Sometimes it makes my left profile weak.

I like my slender body,
Sometimes it makes me confident,
Sometimes I wish for my curves to be
evident.

I like my imperfect grammar,
Sometimes it's an experiment or technique
Sometimes it makes my language critique

With one eye,
I continue to accept myself more.
With the other eye,
I continue to improve myself more.

Part of Me

A part of me is a dreamer,
Another part is a rational being.

A part of me believes in stuff and manifests,
Another part understands the math.

A part of me wants to live bigger than life,
Another part of me just cares about my
parents' pride.

A part of me deserves to achieve everything,
Another part of me navigates reality well.

A part of me is a little bit sad,
And no part of me wants to live with regrets.

Cries With Different Tears

I am clothed,
Yet I cry for more outfits.
There are kids with torn clothes,
Crying for survival.

The cry is not the same.

I have a dad who doesn't
Allow me to sleepover.
There are daughters who can't sleep
As their dad is not around.

The cry is not the same.

I am sad as I have dreams
That I can't pursue.
There are people who don't have time
To dream and feel.

The cry is not the same…

Yes, my misery is still worth the cries,
But at least I have reasons to wipe my tears.

Nothing is the Same

84

Every day passes by,
and nothing changes.

Yet now, when I look back,
my diary is filled with vivid pages.

The days are still usual,
and the nights feel lame.

But now, when I look back,
nothing is the same.

I Now

I won't say I miss you,
But I now take care of myself more.

I won't say I can't sleep at night,
But I now write in my diary often.

I won't say I need you back,
But I now have learned to love myself.

I won't say I cry sometimes,
But I now do things that make me smile.

I won't say anything at all,
But I now write poetry more.

Make A Choice

Make a choice:
Do you want to be loved
or be someone's beloved?

Make a choice:
Do you want to be successful
or witness their success?

Make a choice:
Do you want to be comfortable
or make them feel comfortable?

Make a choice:
Do you want to be happy
or do you want them to be happy?

Make a choice:
Do you want to make decisions for you
or let others make one for you?

Will Not Take You To Bliss

Pursuing your goals
Will not take you to bliss,
In fact, it will snatch away everything
That could bring you near to bliss.

Pursuit of your goals
Is nothing more than "less"—

Less sleep
Will make you weep.

Less time with loved ones,
No rest and longer runs.

Less moments of peace
Will take you on roads that are steep.

Less friends, more peers;
Hard times overcoming all the fears.

Unending lust for success,
Making you unstoppable for real.

If I think a little longer,
It makes me ponder this:
The hustle culture—
Is it a curse or bliss?
Because—

Is success worth the sacrifice?
Are sleepless nights worth the dreams?
Is love for your dreams worth the hatred
you'll receive?
Is the view from the top worth the hike?

And when reading this poem,
If you hate me already.
Trust me, you'll die with a
Goddamn story!

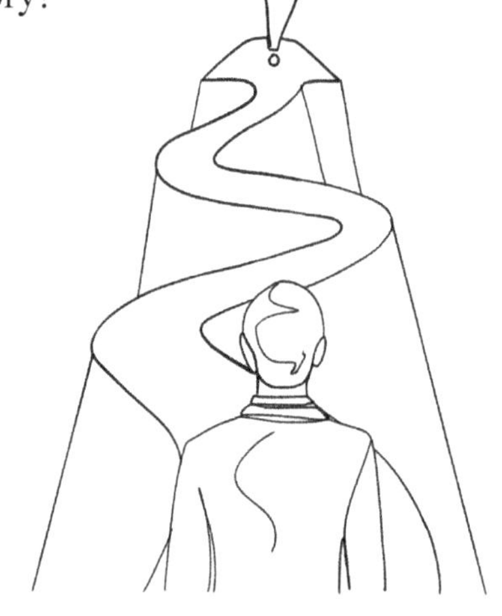

War-Torn Skies

Sky is blue,
It can be a hundred different shades.

But all till the sun is there,
After that, it's just a dark arcade.

But the darkness is not the same for all,
Sometimes it's raining, sometimes snowing.

But what about those,
When the nights are sparkling?

Not with crackers,
For the eyes are scared and not shining.

That orange-colored sky is dreadful,
As no authorities are even whining.

Doesn't matter if it's on
either side of the wall,

All the humans are making
the most inhumane call.

Sunsets, I am Restless

As the bird chirps in,
The sun goes down.
I ponder my day,
With coffee in my arm.

It was productive,
Not the best one though.
I healed a little bit,
And avoided
Getting hurt once more.

Once again, I fell in love
With a fictional guy.
It makes me wonder,
Is love then just a lie?

I am a Pawn

Life is a chess,
With boxes drawn.
I am nothing
But one of those pawns.

The field adorned,
Warriors competitive.
But I am first forced to
Take the first initiative.

The game begins,
I play wise.
However, I am still
The one who gets sacrificed.

Fortunately,
When I play smart
And actually go
Beyond a mark.

And then there comes
My enemy,
Helpless, on its knees,

Right in front of me.

I am taught the
Rules of the game.
Neither I kill,
Nor get any fame.

And being alive,
I die in shame,
Gulping my self-respect,
Digesting all my pain.

Even if I reach the
Finishing line,
I am never even
Bothered to be praised.

Without a thought,
I am exchanged.
All my efforts awarded to a
Defeated player, nothing strange.

Room For Improvement

Thinking of a future,
I think of a house,
A room for us,
A room for guests,

And
A room for improvement.
Not just metaphorically,
But in walls and floors.

A place for growth,
With open doors.

A room for plants, paintings, and poems,
A room for life, laughter, and leisure,
A room for words, work, and wealth,
A room for books, breeze, and bliss,
A room for tea, tulips, and trust,
A room for crystals, candles, and care.

I don't seek a life with many rooms,
But I do seek a room with much life.

North Star

Oh, how
Everyone cannot be the
Moon of your life.

The moon that
You can witness
Shining bright
In every phase.

The moon that promises
To show up every night.

And on some unfortunate nights
When it doesn't appear,
You have faith that it will
Show up and dispel all your fears.

Not everyone can be your moon;
Let one of them be a North Star.

The North Star,
Miles far,
The unachievable,

Yet the unforgettable.

The North Star that shines
Every night without an excuse
And guides you through darkness,

A beacon for your muse.
The one who is distant,
Never disconnected,

Indeed the one
Where wishes are never rejected.

Miserable how we can't be
Moon or sunshine of our lives.

But I hope I'll be yours,
And you'll be my
North Star
For the rest of our lives.

Say hello at!

Website: yashvishahharmony.com
Email: yashvi@yashvishahharmony.com
Instagram: @shahyashvii_harmony
Threads: @shahyashvii_harmony
X (Twitter): @shahyashv

www.ingramcontent.com/pod-product-compliance
Lightning Source LLC
Chambersburg PA
CBHW071333140726

47996CB00005B/1959